REVIEW COPY
COURTESY OF
CAPSTONE PRESS

152.14

Rin C. L 2007 Lord

Yellow Umbrella Books are published by Red Brick Learning
7825 Telegraph Road, Bloomington, Minnesota 55438
http://www.redbricklearning.com

Library of Congress Cataloging-in-Publication Data
Ring, Susan.
   Big or small?/by Susan Ring.
   p. cm.
   Summary: "Simple text and photos show that animals can be big or small and can be sorted into groups by their size"—Provided by publisher.
   Includes index.
   ISBN-13: 978-0-7368-5983-7 (hardcover)
   ISBN-10: 0-7368-5983-7 (hardcover)
   ISBN: 0-7368-1692-5 (softcover)
   1. Proportion—Juvenile literature. 2. Size perception—Juvenile literature. I. Title.
QA117.R56 2006
152.14'2—dc22   2005025747

Written by Susan Ring
Developed by Raindrop Publishing

Editorial Director: Mary Lindeen
Editor: Jennifer VanVoorst
Photo Researcher: Wanda Winch
Conversion Assistants: Jenny Marks, Laura Manthe

Photo Credits:
Cover: Grant Woodrow/Image Ideas, Inc; Title Page: Photo 24/Brand X Pictures;
Page 4: Deirdre Barton/Capstone Press; Page 6: Deirdre Barton/Capstone Press;
Page 8: Richard T. Nowitz/Corbis; Page 10: Bill Hilton Jr./Hilton Pond Center;
Page 12: David Pinquoch/Alaska Good Time Charters; Page 14: Melissa Rickers/
USDA Forest Service/Chippewa National Forest; Page 16: Ralf Schmode

1 2 3 4 5 6 11 10 09 08 07 06

Big or Small?

by Susan Ring

Yellow
Umbrella
Books
for early readers

4

This horse is big.

This horse is small.

This bird is big.

This bird is small.

This fish is big.

This fish is small.

Who is big? Who is small?

Index